Willie Nelson

The Outlaw Country King

Jim McCoy

Willie Nelson

Copyright © 2023 by Jim McCoy

1

Table of Content

Willie Nelson

Introduction

A brief biography of Willie Nelson

In Abbott, Texas, on April 29, 1933, Willie Hugh Nelson was born. His grandparents, who reared him, urged him to pursue music. Nelson composed his first song at the age of seven, and he started playing the guitar at an early age. He also started doing stand-ups at neighborhood dances and honky tonks.

Nelson enlisted in the Air Force in 1950. Due to a back problem, he was dismissed after two years of service. Nelson relocated to Nashville, Tennessee, to pursue a career in music after leaving the Air Force. Before he signed a record deal with RCA Records in 1960, he spent several years working as a session musician and songwriter.

Nelson did not have much success in his early solo career. Despite a few modest hits, he was never able to become well-known. But in 1970, he composed "Crazy," a song that went on to become a tremendous hit for Patsy Cline. Nelson went on to write other hit songs as a result, such as "Hello Walls" and "Funny How Time Slips Away."

Nelson came out with his album Shotgun Willie in 1973. His career took a radical swing after this album. It was among the first records by the Outlaw Country movement, which eschewed the Nashville style and went for a rawer, more genuine sound. Shotgun Willie was a critical and financial triumph that catapulted Nelson to stardom.

Nelson's album Red Headed Stranger was published in 1975. This record is regarded as one of the best country records ever released. The concept album revolves around the story of a disillusioned preacher.

Nelson's eerie vocals are featured in the moody, dark record. Red Headed Stranger was a critical and financial hit that solidified Nelson's place in the annals of country music history.

Nelson kept putting out well-received albums in the 1970s and 1980s. He started acting as well, making appearances in motion pictures including Stagecoach and Honeysuckle Rose. To bring attention to the predicament of American farmers, Nelson hosted the first Farm Aid concert in 1985. Since then, Nelson has carried on with his annual Farm Aid concerts.

Nelson kept making records and going on tours in the 1990s and 2000s. In addition, he put out some well-received albums, such as Across the Borderline (1993), Willie Nelson and Friends (1986), and Stardust (1978). Nelson has kept up his political and activist activities. He has voiced opinions on matters including legalizing drugs, animal rights, and environmental preservation.

One of the most recognizable and significant characters in country music is Nelson. He has sold over 40 million records globally and put out over 90 albums. In addition, he has received other honors, such as 23 Country Music Association Awards and 10 Grammy Awards. Nelson is a genuine American icon, and people all around the world are still inspired and entertained by his music.

The Legacy of Willie Nelson

One of the most adored and esteemed people in country music is Willie Nelson. He is renowned for his advocacy, skill as a songwriter, and distinctive musical style. Nelson has had a significant influence on country music, and future generations will be inspired and amused by his legacy.

Nelson is a real legend, and millions of people have been impacted by his music. He is a living legend who has made incalculable contributions to the genre of country music.

His sound and influence on country music

One of the most recognizable and significant characters in country music is Willie Nelson. For for than 60 years, his distinct musical approach has contributed to defining the genre. Nelson's music is renowned for its easygoing, carefree vibe and combines elements of blues, jazz, country, and folk music. His unique vocals, which are distinguished by their relaxed phrasing and nasal twang, are another thing that makes him well-known.

Nelson's musical taste has been influenced by many different musicians, such as Bob Wills, Roy Acuff, and Hank Williams. But he's always been his guy, and his distinct style and viewpoint are reflected in his music. Nelson frequently delivers his songs with a sense of humor and compassion, and they frequently deal with themes of love, sorrow, and redemption.

Nelson has had a significant influence on country music. The Outlaw Country movement, which revolted against the polished Nashville sound of the 1960s and 1970s, included him among its pioneers. A new generation of country musicians who were more focused on experimentation and authenticity than on financial success were influenced by Nelson's music.

Along with being a supporter of other musicians, Nelson helped establish the careers of other well-known country singers, such as Kris Kristofferson, Waylon

Jennings, and Merle Haggard. In addition, Nelson has worked with musicians from many other genres, such as U2, Bob Dylan, and Frank Sinatra.

Both fans and critics have complimented Nelson's music for its emotional connection, honesty, and sincerity. He is a true American icon, and people all over the world are still inspired and entertained by his songs.

Here are a few particular instances of Nelson's influence on country music:

His group, Outlaw Country, was one of the first to revolt against the smooth Nashville sound of the 1960s and 1970s.
A new generation of country musicians who were more focused on experimentation and authenticity than on financial success were influenced by his music.
He has supported and encouraged the careers of numerous successful country

singers, such as Kris Kristofferson, Waylon Jennings, and Merle Haggard.

In addition, he has worked with musicians from many other genres, including U2, Bob Dylan, and Frank Sinatra.

Nelson wrote the following songs, a few of which have had a big influence on country music:

"Crazy" (1961): Nelson wrote this song, which Patsy Cline recorded that year. It soon rose to the top of the charts and helped establish Nelson as a household figure.

"Red Headed Stranger" (1975): This record is regarded as one of the best-ever country releases. Nelson's eerie vocals are included on a concept album about a preacher who has lost his religion.

"Stardust" (1978): Nelson recorded some pop standards with a jazz ensemble for this album. It was a critical and financial triumph that broadened the listener base for Nelson's music.

"Willie Nelson and Friends" (1986): Nelson collaborates with a range of musicians from other genres, such as Ray Charles, Bonnie Raitt, and Johnny Cash. As a result of its critical and commercial success, Nelson's reputation as one of the greatest artists of all time was further cemented.

A great American legend, Willie Nelson's music never fails to uplift and amuse listeners everywhere. For more than 60 years, his distinct musical style and dedication to authenticity have contributed to the definition of country music. Nelson has had an incalculable influence on the genre, and his legacy will inspire and amuse people for many years to come.

His charitable giving and activism

In addition to being a fervent activist and philanthropist, Willie Nelson has devoted his life to serving others. Nelson has been an outspoken supporter of several issues, including the legalization of drugs, animal rights, and environmental preservation. Through his advocacy and singing, he has also helped generate millions of dollars for charitable causes.

Protection of the Environment

Nelson is a major proponent of environmental protection. He is an outspoken supporter of sustainable agriculture and renewable energy. Nelson has also made statements opposing the fossil fuel sector and climate change. Nelson established the Willie Nelson and Friends Biodiesel Company in 2007, which manufactures and markets fuel made from biodiesel. He has also advocated for environmental causes through his music. Nelson's CD Heroes, which includes songs about heroes and environmental campaigners, was released in 2012.

Animal Welfare

Nelson is a fervent supporter of animal rights as well. He has made statements opposing factory farming and animal abuse. Nelson has additionally contributed to animal protection groups including Farm Sanctuary and the Humane Society. Nelson made the "The Love of Horses" music video available in 2014 to bring attention to horse slaughter.

Drug Legalization
Nelson is a strong supporter of legalizing drugs as well. Like alcohol and tobacco, he thinks narcotics should be controlled and subject to taxes. Nelson has also expressed his views on the negative effects of the drug war. Nelson established the Willie Nelson and Friends Country Throwdown in 2015 as a fundraiser performance to support the change of drug laws.

Philanthropy

Nelson's activism and songs have helped to raise millions of dollars for charitable causes. To bring attention to the predicament of American farmers, Nelson hosted the first Farm Aid concert in 1985. Since its start, Farm Aid has raised more than $50 million. In addition, Nelson has contributed to numerous other charitable organizations, such as the NAACP, the Salvation Army, and the Red Cross.

Here are a few particular instances of Nelson's charitable giving and activism:

To bring attention to the predicament of American farmers, Nelson hosted the first Farm Aid concert in 1985. Since its start, Farm Aid has raised more than $50 million. Nelson established the charity Willie Nelson and Friends Foundation in 1987. It promotes a range of causes, such as animal rights, environmental preservation, and changes to drug laws.

Nelson established the Willie Nelson and Friends Biodiesel Company in 2007, which manufactures and markets fuel made from biodiesel.

Nelson's CD Heroes, which includes songs about heroes and environmental campaigners, was released in 2012.

Nelson made the "The Love of Horses" music video available in 2014 to bring attention to horse slaughter.

Nelson established the Willie Nelson and Friends Country Throwdown in 2015 as a fundraiser performance to support the change of drug laws.

Nelson's charitable giving and activism have made a big difference. In addition to raising millions of cash to aid others, he has contributed to the awareness-building of significant concerns. Nelson is a real role model, and we are all inspired by his dedication to social justice.

Chapter 1

Foundation Years

Being Raised In Texas

In Abbott, Texas, on April 29, 1933, Willie Nelson was born. His grandparents, who reared him, urged him to pursue music. Nelson composed his first song at the age of seven, and he started playing the guitar at an early age. He also started doing stand-ups at neighborhood dances and honky tonks.

Texas's strong feeling of community and rich musical legacy influenced Nelson's early years. Many Texas musicians, such as Hank Williams, Bob Wills, and Ernest Tubb, had an impact on him. Nelson's granddad was a skilled violinist and taught him a lot about music as well.

Nelson did not always have an easy life in Texas. His family had a difficult time making ends meet while he was growing up during the Great Depression. Nelson, though, has always talked positively of his Texas upbringing. He attributes his development as a musician and a person to the people and culture of the state.

Texas music and community
Texas has a lengthy and vibrant history in music. Many musical styles are found throughout the state, such as rock and roll, jazz, blues, and country. Nelson has stated that as a young artist, the variety of Texas music had a significant influence on him.

Nelson also attributes the growth of his musical career to Texas's strong feeling of community. Even in his early career, he claimed, he could always find a venue in Texas to perform music.

Texas-inspired songs by Nelson

Nelson's Texas upbringing had a big impact on his music. His songs frequently touch on themes of redemption, love, and loss. His songs are renowned for having a carefree, laid-back vibe.

Red Headed Stranger, one of Nelson's best-known albums, is a concept record about a minister who has lost his religion. Numerous songs on the album discuss the people and culture of Texas, where the CD is located.

"On the Road Again," one of Nelson's songs, is another illustration of his Texas influence. The freedom to roam and the open road are celebrated in this song. Many people connect this song to Texas and its famous freeways.

Taking up guitar playing

Willie Nelson's grandfather, Ira Doyle Nelson, taught him how to play the guitar when he was very little. Ira was a gifted guitarist and fiddler who was always glad to teach Willie new skills.

When Willie was six years old, his grandfather handed him his first guitar. Willie was drawn to the little Sears and Roebuck guitar right away. He would practice for hours on end and picked up the fundamentals of playing the guitar very quickly.

Apart from gaining knowledge from his grandfather, Willie acquired a great deal of guitar-playing expertise by listening to other artists. He would frequently attend neighborhood dances and honky tonks to see the bands perform. Along with learning songs from his favorite artists, like Hank

Williams and Bob Wills, he would also listen to the radio.

Willie was born to be a musician, and he picked up the guitar quite quickly. Despite being self-taught, he was able to hone his guitar technique. His utilization of intriguing chord progressions and easygoing tone are what define his guitar playing.

Willie's usage of arpeggios is one of the things that sets his guitar playing apart from others. Broken chords are called arpeggios, and Willie is an expert at playing them. He frequently employs arpeggios to produce a more intriguing and melodic tone.

The usage of open tunings by Willie is another characteristic that sets his guitar playing apart. When all the strings are tuned to open chords, this is referred to as an open tuning. To produce a more resonant and mellow sound, Willie frequently chooses open tunings.

The way that Willie plays the guitar has greatly influenced country music. The Outlaw Country movement, which revolted against the polished Nashville sound of the 1960s and 1970s, included him among its pioneers. Nelson's guitar style paved the way for a new wave of country musicians who were less concerned with mainstream success and more with authenticity and innovation.

Willie Nelson picked up the following guitar-playing tips from his grandfather, Ira Doyle Nelson:

the fundamentals of playing the guitar, including how to handle the instrument, pluck the notes, and form chords.
How to play notes and read music.
How to perform open tunings and arpeggios.
How to hone a distinct and original guitar style.

Willie Nelson also gained a great deal of knowledge about playing the guitar by routinely practicing and listening to other guitarists. Despite being a self-taught musician, he is among the most accomplished and well-known guitarists in country music.

Willie Nelson's guitar playing has influenced country music in the following ways:

The Outlaw Country movement, which revolted against the polished Nashville sound of the 1960s and 1970s, included him among its pioneers.
His guitar style paved the way for a new wave of country musicians who were less concerned with mainstream success and more with experimentation and authenticity.
Numerous other country guitarists have been influenced by his usage of arpeggios and open tunings.
He's become one of the most well-known and significant guitarists in country music

thanks to his distinctive style of playing the guitar.

People throughout the world are still inspired and entertained by the guitar playing of Willie Nelson, a true legend of the instrument. Future generations of guitarists will be motivated and inspired by his legacy.

His initial musical endeavors

At a young age, Willie Nelson started his musical career. When he was just a youngster, he started playing at neighborhood dances and honky tonks, having learned to play the guitar from his grandfather. Nelson enlisted in the Air Force in 1950, but his back issues caused him to be released two years later. Nelson relocated to Nashville, Tennessee, to pursue a career in music after leaving the Air Force.

Nelson had a rough time in his early years in Nashville. As a musician and songwriter, he had difficulty finding employment. Additionally, he struggled to get his music recorded. Nelson, though, never gave up on his goal of being a well-known artist.

Nelson landed his first recording contract with RCA Records in 1960. In 1962, he published And Then I Wrote, his debut album. Despite not being a commercial hit, the album featured some of Nelson's early hits, including "Crazy" and "Hello Walls."

In 1961, Nelson's breakthrough performance was when Patsy Cline recorded his song "Crazy." Nelson became well-known after the song became a big hit. Following the popularity of "Crazy," Nelson was able to convince other musicians to record more of his tunes. Also, he started to see greater success with his recordings. Nelson released Shotgun Willie, his album, in 1965. This record is regarded as one of the Outlaw Country movement's early records. A new subgenre of country music known as "Outlaw Country" emerged in opposition to the polished Nashville sound of the 1960s. A new generation of country music lovers was drawn to Nelson's music because it was more genuine and unadulterated.

Nelson's Years in Outlaw Country

During his career, Nelson's Outlaw Country years were among his most fruitful and prosperous periods. He put out some highly regarded albums, such as Willie and the Wheel (1980), Stardust (1978), and Red Headed Stranger (1975). Among the most well-known Nelson songs were included on these albums: "Blue Eyes Crying in the Rain," "To All the Girls I've Loved Before," and "On the Road Again."

Nelson's Rebel Other country musicians like Kris Kristofferson, Merle Haggard, and

Waylon Jennings were greatly influenced by country music. Nelson and these musicians are referred to as the "Outlaw Gang." The Outlaw Gang contributed to transforming the sound of country music, giving it a more genuine and approachable vibe for a younger audience.

Nelson's Achievements in the 1990s and 1980s

Nelson remained successful into the 1980s and 1990s. He put out several hit albums, such as Highwayman (1985), Always on My Mind (1982), and Across the Borderline (1993). He also carried on giving sold-out performances across the country on lengthy tours.

Nelson hosted the inaugural Farm Aid concert in 1985. A benefit concert called Farm Aid raises money to support American farmers. Since 1985, Nelson has arranged a Farm Aid concert each year.

Nelson has contributed to several other philanthropic initiatives as well. He is a fervent supporter of animal rights and environmental preservation. Additionally, he has voiced opposition to the war on drugs.

Nelson's Heritage

One of the most recognizable and significant characters in the history of country music is Willie Nelson. He has sold over 40 million records globally and put out over 90 albums. In addition, he has received other honors, such as 23 Country Music Association Awards and 10 Grammy Awards.

Fans of all ages have been drawn to Nelson's music because it crosses genre boundaries. His approach is easygoing and laid back, and he is well-known for writing

Willie Nelson

catchy yet deep songs. He also has a
distinctive voice.

Chapter 2

Ascent to Fame

RCA Records signing

Willie Nelson originally got a record contract with RCA Records in 1960. Nelson's career saw a significant turning point at this time. Signing with one of the largest record labels in the world, RCA, signaled to Nelson that he had at last made it as an artist.

Before signing with RCA, Nelson had been trying unsuccessfully for some years to make it in Nashville. Although he had put out a few singles, none of them had been really popular. Though he had written a few songs that other singers had recorded, such as Patsy Cline's "Crazy," he had not yet found any success on his own.

After making an impression on the label's chief of A&R, Chet Atkins, Nelson signed with RCA. Nelson's distinctive vocal style and creative abilities pleased Atkins. Nelson's willingness to stand out from the other country singers of the era was another quality that appealed to him.

Nelson's And Then I Wrote was his debut album for RCA. 1961 saw the publication of the album, which included some of Nelson's early hits like "Crazy" and "Hello Walls." Although the album did not achieve commercial success, it did contribute to Nelson's recognition as a gifted songwriter.

Throughout the 1960s, Nelson put out several albums for RCA, but he never found much financial success. His music deviated too much from the popular Nashville sound of the day. Nelson, however, never lost hope in his idea and carried on creating and

Recording The Music He Was Passionate About.
Nelson's album Red Headed Stranger was published in 1975. A significant turning point in his career was this record. The concept album, which told the story of a preacher who has lost his religion, included several moody and atmospheric tracks. As a result of the album's critical and financial success, Nelson rose to prominence in the country music industry.

Nelson kept putting out popular albums for RCA in the 1970s and 1980s. In addition, he rose to prominence as a touring performer, selling out arenas across the globe. Nelson is today regarded as one of the most significant individuals in the history of country music because of his popularity, which altered the sound of the genre.

The Effect of RCA on Nelson's Career
The major influence on Nelson's career came from RCA. He was able to record his songs and release them to a larger audience thanks to the label. Nelson became one of the biggest performers in country music thanks in part to RCA's promotion of his work.

There were problems with Nelson's connection with RCA at times. He and the label's executives frequently disagreed on his artistic vision. Nelson, though, never wavered from his commitment to his music or himself. He never allowed RCA to pressure him to give up on his creative principles.

Nelson started recording for his own company, Lucky Dog Records, after leaving RCA in the 1990s. He did, however, maintain a cordial connection with RCA, and

The label put out Multiple Compilation CDs Featuring his Music.

An important part of Nelson's career was RCA. He had wanted to be a successful musician his entire life, and the label helped him realize this goal. Nelson is today regarded as one of the most significant individuals in the history of country music because of the impact his songs have on the genre.

An important part of Nelson's career was RCA. He had wanted to be a successful musician his entire life, and the label helped him realize this goal. Nelson is today regarded as one of the most significant individuals in the history of country music because of the impact his songs have on the genre.

Composing hits for other musicians

One of the most successful composers in the history of country music is Willie Nelson. Several of the more than 2,000 songs he has composed have gone on to become hits for other musicians. Nelson is well-known for his songs' straightforward melodies, appealing hooks, and sincere lyrics. Themes of love, grief, and redemption are frequently addressed.

In 1961, Nelson's first significant hit song was covered by Patsy Cline as "Crazy." Nelson became well-known thanks in part to the song, which was a big smash. Nelson has since penned numerous other successes for various musicians, such as:

Faron Young's song "Hello Walls"
Billy Walker's "Funny How Time Slips Away"
Roy Orbison's "Pretty Paper"
Lynn Anderson's "One Day at a Time"
As said by Willie Nelson and Julio Iglesias in "To All the Girls I've Loved Before"

Willie Nelson

Willie Nelson's song "On the Road Again"
Presley's "Always on My Mind"
The Highwaymen's "Highwayman"
Emmylou Harris and Willie Nelson's "Across the Borderline"
Numerous musicians, including pop stars, jazz greats, and country singers, have recorded Nelson's tunes. In addition, a lot of movies and TV series have used his tunes.

There are several reasons behind Nelson's songwriter's success. He is, first and foremost, a talented songwriter with a gift for crafting memorable songs and profound lyrics. Second, Nelson's compositions frequently address universal issues that connect with listeners because he has a profound understanding of human nature. Third, Nelson has had the good fortune to have some of the biggest stars in music record his tunes.

The following are a few instances of Willie Nelson's popular songs that other musicians have covered:

Patsy Cline's song "Crazy" is a prime illustration of Nelson's compositional prowess. It features a straightforward melody, an appealing hook, and open lyrics about a lady going crazy about a man. Faron Young's poignant ballad "Hello Walls" tells the story of a lonely man conversing with his empty home. Over the years, other performers have covered one of Nelson's most well-known songs.

Billy Walker's "Funny How Time Slips Away": This song is a sentimental ballad about time passing. Listeners have been moved by this lovely melody for years.

The beloved Christmas song "Pretty Paper" by Roy Orbison tells the story of a destitute guy who sells paper on the streets. This endearing tune has become a holiday mainstay.

Lynn Anderson's uplifting ballad "One Day at a Time" is about living each day as it comes. Many people have found solace in this message of hope during trying times. Julio Iglesias and Willie Nelson's song "To All the Girls I've Loved Before" is a lovely ballad about a man's love for every woman he has ever loved. Over the years, numerous singers have covered this lovely song.

Willie Nelson's song "On the Road Again" is an anthem for the free spirit. The song is about the excitement of being on the open road and the delight of traveling. Elvis Presley's "Always on My Mind" is a timeless love ballad about a man lamenting the loss of the woman he once held dear. It is among the all-time greatest hits and has been covered by numerous musicians throughout the years. The Highwaymen sing a duet called "Highwayman" with fellow country music icons Johnny Cash, Waylon Jennings, and

Kris Kristofferson. The song tells the story of four bandits riding into the horizon.

Emmylou Harris and Willie Nelson's "Across the Borderline": This lovely ballad speaks about a love that knows no boundaries. For years, audiences have found resonance in this song that exudes love and hope.

One of the most successful composers in the history of country music is Willie Nelson. Several of the more than 2,000 songs he has composed have gone on to become hits for other musicians. Nelson is well-known for his songs' straightforward melodies, appealing hooks, and sincere lyrics. Themes of love, grief, and redemption are frequently addressed. Many things contribute to Nelson's success as a songwriter, such as his exceptional songwriting abilities, his profound knowledge of human nature, and the fact that some of the biggest names in music have recorded his songs. Nelson wrote timeless classics that audiences will love for a very long time.

His breakthrough hits, such as "Crazy" and "Red Headed Stranger"

One of the most recognizable and significant characters in the history of country music is Willie Nelson. He has sold over 40 million records globally and put out over 90 albums. Nelson is well-known for his unusual voice, easygoing demeanor, and knack for penning catchy yet thought-provoking songs.

The two greatest hits Nelson had upon his breakout were "Crazy" and "Red Headed Stranger." Nelson became a household name in the country music industry thanks to these songs, which also served to define his career.

Crazy

Nelson wrote the song "Crazy" in 1961. When Patsy Cline recorded it for the first time in 1961, it swiftly rose to the top of the charts. The song is about a crazy woman who can't stop thinking about a man. It's a melancholic tune with eerie lyrics and a gloomy, atmospheric feel. 1962 saw the publication of Nelson's rendition of "Crazy" on his debut album, And Then I Wrote. Though it is a more relaxed and laid-back rendition of the song than Cline's, it is nonetheless powerful and poignant. Nelson's song "Crazy" is among his most well-known ones. Over the years, some performers have covered it, including Barbra Streisand, Frank Sinatra, and Elvis Presley. Additionally, the song has appeared in a lot of movies and TV series.

Red-Headed stranger
Nelson released his concept album "Red Headed Stranger" in 1975. The story of a pastor who has lost faith is told in the album. It's a somber and gloomy record with a

distinct tone that sets it apart from other releases of the period.

The album's lead single, "The Preacher's Journey," is an eerie ballad. One of Nelson's most well-known songs, it's a strong and poignant tune.

"Blue Eyes Crying in the Rain," "To All the Girls I've Loved Before," and "Sunday Morning Coming Down" are a few more standout tracks on the album. Red Headed Stranger is one of the best country albums ever recorded because of these songs, all of which are masterfully written and sung.

Important Effect of "Crazy" and "Red-headed stranger"

Red Headed Stranger" and "Crazy" had a significant effect on Nelson's career. Both his sound and his rise to prominence in the country music industry were shaped by these tunes.

The timeless country ballad "Crazy" has delighted fans for many years. This song has endured throughout time and is one of Nelson's most well-known compositions.

The innovative record "Red Headed Stranger" significantly altered the sound of country music. It's a somber and gloomy record with a distinct tone that sets it apart from other releases of the period. The record is regarded as one of the best country albums ever created and is a masterpiece.

Chapter 3

Outlaw country

The Outlaw Country Movement

The Nashville sound, which dominated country music at the time and was polished and commercialized, gave rise to the Outlaw Country movement in the early 1970s. The raw, genuine music, rebellious attitudes, and determination to push the boundaries of country music were hallmarks of Outlaw Country singers.

Among the forerunners of the Outlaw Country trend was Willie Nelson. His approach was easygoing and low back, and he was well known for his distinctive voice and ability to produce meaningful yet popular songs. Nelson's upbringing in Texas and his struggles as a struggling Nashville songwriter had a big impact on his music.

Nelson's album Red Headed Stranger was published in 1975. This record is regarded as one of the Outlaw Country movement's foundational records. This concept album, which tells the story of a preacher who has lost his religion, comprises a lot of eerie and disturbing tracks. As a result of the album's critical and financial success, Nelson rose to prominence in the country music industry. Kris Kristofferson, Waylon Jennings, Johnny Cash, and Merle Haggard are a few other well-known Outlaw Country performers. The 1970s and 1980s saw a shift in the sound of country music thanks to the efforts of these musicians, who were all renowned for their unadulterated and genuine music.

Country music was greatly influenced by the Outlaw Country movement. It opened the door for a new generation of country musicians who weren't scared to be distinctive and helped revive the classic honky-tonk sound of the genre. A larger audience was able to enjoy country music thanks in part to the Outlaw Country movement.

The following are some of the Outlaw Country movement's salient features:

a genuine, unprocessed sound as opposed to the era's refined, commercialized Nashville sound.
a disobedient mindset and a readiness to test the limits of country music.
a concentration on classic themes in country music, such as love, grief, and redemption.
utilization of appealing hooks and straightforward tunes.
a readiness to include elements of other musical genres, such as blues and rock & roll.
All of these qualities may be heard in Willie Nelson's music. His sound is unadulterated and genuine, and he doesn't hesitate to

challenge the conventions of country music. Nelson is well-known for his straightforward melodies and memorable hooks, and his songs frequently touch on classic country music topics. The blues and rock & roll have also affected Nelson's work.

There is no denying Nelson's influence on the Outlaw Country movement and country music in general. He is among the most significant and influential people in the annals of country music. For many years, his music has influenced the style of country music.

Here are some examples of Willie Nelson's songs that are considered to be Outlaw Country classics:

"Crazy"
"Hello Walls"
"Funny How Time Slips Away"
"Pretty Paper"
"One Day at a Time"

"To All the Girls I've Loved Before"
"On the Road Again"
"Always on My Mind"
"Highwayman"
"Across the Borderline"

Nelson's raw, genuine sound, rebellious spirit, and determination to challenge the boundaries of country music are all evident in these tunes. These songs have become some of the most well-known and iconic country songs of all time, and they are all exquisitely written and performed.

A true country music legend is Willie Nelson. His music has influenced country music for many years, and he is considered one of the forerunners of the Outlaw Country movement. Nelson is a genuine artist who has never shied away from being authentic, and millions of people all over the world have been inspired and amused by his music.

Nelson's part in the movement

Among the forerunners of the Outlaw
Country trend was Willie Nelson. His music
was recognized for its authenticity and
rawness, and he was renowned for his
defiant demeanor and determination to push
the frontiers of country music. Nelson's
upbringing in Texas and his struggles as a
struggling Nashville songwriter had a big
impact on his music.

Nelson was dissatisfied with the Nashville
sound, the polished and commercialized
kind of country music that ruled the
business in the early 1970s. Nelson was
inspired by the rising outlaw movement at
the time and wanted to create music that
was more real and unadulterated.

The Nashville sound sparked the outlaw
movement, which was distinguished by its
rebellious spirit and openness to trying out

novel sounds. Songwriters in the Outlaw Country genre were not hesitant to tackle contentious subjects and frequently utilized their music as a platform to convey their social and political opinions.

Nelson prominently led the outlaw movement. Throughout the 1970s, he put out several albums that contributed to the definition of the genre, such as Willie and the Wheel (1980), Stardust (1978), and Red Headed Stranger (1975). Nelson became one of the biggest names in country music because of these critically and commercially successful albums.

Nelson's music had a significant impact on the revival of the classic honky-tonk sound of country music. Nelson frequently used steel guitars and fiddles, two common rural instruments, in his straightforward and cheerful tunes. Nelson's usage of slide guitar and his deep vocals were two more examples of the blues' profound influence on his music.

Nelson was well-known not only for his singing but also for his rebellious demeanor and eagerness to push the envelope in the country music industry. Nelson was a strong opponent of the Nashville establishment and frequently voiced his disapproval of the commercialization of the music business. Nelson frequently smoked marijuana on stage and was a fervent supporter of legalizing the drug.

Nelson became well-liked by lovers of country music thanks to his renegade persona. Nelson's willingness to be unusual and his genuineness drew his fans. A newer generation of country music fans who desired something beyond the staged and packaged Nashville sound also found Nelson's music appealing.

Nelson had a big part in the outlaw movement. His songs contributed to defining the outlaw sound, and he was one of the genre's pioneers. Nelson's work also contributed to the revival of the classic honky-tonk sound and increased accessibility to country music for a larger audience.

Here are a few particular instances of Nelson's involvement with the outlaw movement:
Nelson was among the first musicians in the country music genre to criticize the Nashville sound.
Nelson's music was honest and unvarnished, and it tackled contentious subjects head-on.
Nelson was an outspoken opponent of the industry's emphasis on consumerism.
Nelson was a fervent supporter of legalizing marijuana.
Nelson became well-liked by lovers of country music thanks to his renegade persona.
There is no denying Nelson's influence on both the outlaw movement and country music in general. He is among the most significant and influential people in the

annals of country music. For many years, his music has influenced the style of country music.

Nelson is still performing now; he is going on frequent tours and releasing new tracks. He is a genuine country music icon, and future generations will be inspired and amused by his legacy.

His records "Stardust" and "Red Headed Stranger"

In the annals of country music, Willie Nelson's albums Red Headed Stranger (1975) and Stardust (1978) are among the most well-regarded and impactful. In addition, they are two of Nelson's most well-liked and prosperous albums, and they have contributed to his reputation as one of the best country music artists of all time.

Red-Headed Stranger
The concept album Red Headed Stranger
tells the story of a pastor who has lost
religion. It's an eerie, moody record with a
distinct sound that set it apart from other
albums being released at the time. Nelson
wrote many of the songs on the album,
including "Blue Eyes Crying in the Rain," "To
All the Girls I've Loved Before," and
"Sunday Morning Coming Down." These
songs are regarded as his masterpieces.
Nelson's personal experiences as a
composer in Nashville served as the basis
for Red Headed Stranger. He wanted to
create an album that was more
unadulterated and genuine since he was
dissatisfied with the overly commercialized
Nashville sound of the day. Nelson also
desired to examine his skepticism and
anxieties over religion and God.

When Red Headed Stranger was first
released, it was a critical and financial
success. Considered one of the best-ever

country albums, it was awarded the 1976 Country Music Association Award for Album of the Year.

Stardust
Nelson recorded the pop standards album Stardust in 1978. Compared to his earlier albums, which mainly featured country music, this one was different. Nelson's rendition of these standards, nevertheless, was every bit as lovely and poignant as his country hits.
Nelson's passion for pop music served as inspiration for the Stardust album. He wanted to honor the musicians he grew up listening to, including Bing Crosby and Frank Sinatra, with this record. Nelson also wanted to demonstrate his ability to sing a wide range of musical styles.
When Stardust was first released, it was a critical and financial success. It is regarded as one of the best albums of all time and received the 1979 Grammy Award for Best Male Country Vocal Performance.

The Legend of "Stardust" and "Red Headed Stranger"

In the history of country music, two of the most significant albums are Red Headed Stranger and Stardust. They opened the way for a new generation of country musicians who weren't scared to be different and helped define the outlaw country movement of the 1970s.

These CDs feature some of Nelson's most vulnerable and honest music. Nelson conveys his uncertainties and anxieties via relevant and poignant songs. Nelson has become one of the most adored and respected characters in country music because of his openness and vulnerability. Nelson's most well-known and prosperous albums are Red Headed Stranger and Stardust. They have produced multiple hit singles and have sold millions of copies globally. Critics have also given these

Willie Nelson

albums high marks for their production value, performances, and songwriting. Every lover of country music should listen to Red Headed Stranger and Stardust. These two albums rank among the best of all time, and they have greatly influenced the genre.

Chapter 4

Achievement in Business

His achievements during the 1980s and 1990s

Even though Willie Nelson was already well-known in the country music industry in the 1970s, his popularity only increased in the 1980s and 1990s. During this period, he put out several successful albums, such as Across the Borderline (1993), Willie and the Wheel (1980), Stardust (1978), and Always on My Mind (1982). Successful duets like "To All the Girls I've Loved Before" featuring Julio Iglesias and "Highwayman" featuring Johnny Cash, Waylon Jennings, and Kris Kristofferson were among the songs he co-wrote with other musicians.

Nelson's accomplishments in the 1980s and 1990s were the result of several things. First of all, his music was still inventive and new. He didn't hesitate to try out new genres, and a lot of his songs dealt with contentious subjects. Second, Nelson had a great rapport with his audience as a charming performer. His easygoing demeanor and a good sense of humor were well-known. Thirdly, Nelson composed a great deal of his hits and was a prolific songwriter. He was also well-known for adding his special touch to songs that he covered by other musicians.

A closer examination of Nelson's achievements throughout the 1980s and 1990s can be found here:

The 1980s
Nelson had a great start to the 1980s. His 1978 album Stardust was a big hit, both economically and critically. Nelson covered

several great pop tunes for the album, including "Stardust" and "Blue Skies." Nelson was able to reach a wider audience because of his inventive and modern renditions of these classics.

Nelson and Waylon Jennings collaborated on their follow-up album, Willie and the Wheel, released in 1980. The album, which included the smash singles "Mama Don't Let Your Babies Grow Up to Be Cowboys" and "Good Hearted Woman," was a critical and commercial success.

Throughout the 1980s, Nelson kept putting out successful albums; among them was The IRS Tapes: Who'll Buy My Memories? (1992), City of New Orleans (1984), and Always on My Mind (1982). Successful duets like "To All the Girls I've Loved Before" featuring Julio Iglesias and "Highwayman" featuring Johnny Cash, Waylon Jennings, and Kris Kristofferson were among the songs he co-wrote with other musicians.

The Nineties

Nelson remained successful far into the 1990s. During this period, he put out several successful albums, such as Across the Borderline (1993), Teatro (1998), and Rainbow Connection (1999). Along with this, he worked on hit duets with other musicians, including "The Maker" with Bonnie Raitt and "Pancho and Lefty" with Merle Haggard.

Nelson's involvement in a variety of other endeavors coincided with his music career during the 1990s. He was the lead actor in the 1980 picture Honeysuckle Rose and the author of Willie: An Autobiography (1993). He also started to speak out in favor of environmental preservation and the legalization of marijuana.

His partnerships with other creatives

One of the most active collaborators in the history of music is Willie Nelson. He has collaborated on albums and duets with a variety of performers, including pop singers, jazz musicians, and legendary country musicians. Among his most illustrious partnerships are:

Julio Iglesias and "To All the Girls I've Loved Before" (1984)
"Highwayman" featuring Kris Kristofferson, Waylon Jennings, and Johnny Cash (1985)
Merle Haggard in "Pancho and Lefty" (1983)
Emmylou Harris's "On the Road Again" and Bonnie Raitt's "The Maker" (1992)
Ray Charles in "Seven Spanish Angels" (1984)
Waylon Jennings in "Good Hearted Woman" (1980)
Waylon Jennings and "Mammas Don't Let Your Babies Grow Up to Be Cowboys" (1975)
Waylon Jennings and "Luckenbach, Texas (Back to the Basics of Love)" (1977)
"Roll Me Up and Smoke Me When I Die" with Snoop Dogg, Kris Kristofferson, and

Jamey Johnson (2012) "Across the Borderline" with Emmylou Harris (1993) "Crazy" with Patsy Cline (1961) and "Pretty Paper" featuring Roy Orbison (1962) Nelson has received recognition for his ability to bring out the best in his partners and for the range of his collaborations. He's also been acknowledged for his role in bringing up-and-coming musicians to a larger public. For instance, his partnership with Julio Iglesias facilitated Iglesias's debut on the American scene.

Nelson's partnerships have yielded positive commercial results as well. Not only have his collaborative albums been successful, but many of his duets have also topped the charts. For instance, Willie and the Wheel, his joint record with Waylon Jennings, was a big hit and took home the 1980 Country Music Association Record of the Year Award.

Nelson's collaborations are evidence of his adaptability and his desire to try out new musical styles. They have also contributed to his rise to prominence as one of the world's most well-liked and esteemed musicians.

Here are a few more noteworthy projects that Willie Nelson worked on:

Billy Walker in "Funny How Time Slips Away" (1961), Lynn Anderson in "One Day at a Time" (1970), and Faron Young in "Hello Walls" (1961)
Ray Price, "Yesterday When I Was Young" (1970)
Waylon Jennings and "My Heroes Have Always Been Cowboys" (1976)
Toby Keith, "Mamas Don't Let Your Babies Grow Up to Be Cowboys" (2003)
Elvis Presley and "Always on My Mind" (1978)
With Alison Krauss, "To Make You Feel My Love" (1999)

Emmylou Harris and "Angel Flying Too Close to the Ground" (1987)
"Duets II" featuring a range of musicians (2006)
"Willie's Stash, Vol. 1" including a variety of artists (2015) "Heroes" with a variety of artists (2012)
Nelson has collaborated with some of the greatest names in music history, whose relationships have transcended generations. He's become one of the most adored and respected artists in the world because of his openness to try new things and his ability to bring out the best in his partners.

His Farm Aid events

Willie Nelson has a strong commitment to supporting rural communities and family farmers. Nelson established Farm Aid, a nonprofit that raises funds and public awareness to assist American family farmers, in 1985.

The 1980s farm crisis, which was brought on by some variables such as poor crop prices, high borrowing rates, and a strong US dollar, prompted the founding of Farm Aid. Millions of family farms were lost as a result of the crisis, and rural towns saw a downturn.

Nelson assembled a group of musicians to play at a charity concert in Champaign, Illinois, on September 22, 1985, because he was committed to supporting family farmers. The event raised more than $9 million for family farmers, and it was a great success.

Nelson performed at the inaugural Farm Aid concert among notable performers like Bob Dylan, Billy Joel, Neil Young, John Mellencamp, and others. With a live broadcast on MTV and VH1, the concert was seen by nearly 20 million people.

Since 1985, there have been yearly Farm Aid concerts, with the COVID-19 epidemic preventing 2020 and 2021 from happening. A diverse spectrum of performers, including pop stars, rock bands, and country music icons, have performed at the performances. Several well-known performers who have graced Farm Aid stages include:

Willie Nelson
Neil Young
John Mellencamp
Dave Matthews and Tim Reynolds
Emmylou Harris
Merle Haggard
Bonnie Raitt
Bruce Springsteen
Paul Simon
Tom Petty
Stevie Wonder
Garth Brooks
Bruce Hornsby
Kacey Musgraves
Chris Stapleton

Luke Combs

Since 1985, Farm Aid performances have raised more than $60 million. Family farmers have benefited from the funds in some ways, including:

supplying farmers who have experienced natural calamities or financial difficulties with emergency help.

assisting farmers in making the switch to sustainable farming methods.

encouraging other regional food systems, such as farmers' markets.

promoting laws that help rural areas and family farmers.

Farm Aid concerts are more than just occasions for charitable giving. They provide a chance to spread awareness of the difficulties faced by rural communities and family farmers. Speakers and informational displays educate concertgoers about the problems and what they can do to become involved in the concerts.

Family farmers' lives in the US have been significantly impacted by Farm Aid. The group has promoted the creation of sustainable agricultural methods and assisted in keeping millions of family farmers on their land. Farm Aid has also promoted legislation that assists family farmers and increased public understanding of the difficulties that rural communities and family farmers face.

A real defender of small-town life and family farmers, Willie Nelson is. His time and money have been committed to helping Farm Aid fulfill its goal of promoting the prosperity of family farmers. Nelson's Farm Aid performances have positively impacted millions of people's lives and are still a vital voice for rural areas and family farmers.

Chapter 5

Later Times

His ongoing popularity as a songwriter and performer

One of the most recognizable and significant characters in the history of country music is Willie Nelson. His approach is easygoing and laid back, and he is well-known for writing catchy yet deep songs. He also has a distinctive voice. In addition, Nelson is a very active musician and songwriter who has been touring and putting out new songs well into his eighties.

Many things contribute to Nelson's ongoing success. His music is timeless, to start with. His songs continue to speak to listeners of all ages because they deal with universal topics like love, grief, and redemption.

Nelson is a superb performer, to start with. He has a great ability to engage his audience and produce a unique experience. Thirdly, Nelson writes a lot of songs. Many of the hundreds of songs he has composed have gone on to become classics.

As an Entertainer
Nelson is among the world's most well-liked live performers. His shows are always sold out, and he tours extensively. Nelson's concerts are renowned for their carefree and easygoing vibe. He has a natural ability to connect with the audience and act. Both fans and critics have applauded Nelson's live performances. The magazine Rolling Stone has referred to him as "one of the greatest live performers of all time." Nelson, according to the New York Times, "is a master of the laid-back, conversational delivery."

Nelson gives more than just concerts when he performs live. Fans can also interact with him and his music through these. In between songs, Nelson frequently cracks jokes and stories that foster a sense of camaraderie among his followers.

In Songwriting
Nelson is among the most prolific songwriters in the annals of country music. Many of the hundreds of songs he has composed have gone on to become classics. Nelson is well-known for his songs' straightforward melodies, memorable hooks, and poignant lyrics.

Nelson's most well-known tunes include the following:

"Crazy"
"Hello Walls"
"Funny How Time Slips Away"
"One Day at a Time"
"To All the Girls I've Loved Before"

"On the Road Again"
"Always on My Mind"
"Highwayman"
"Across the Borderline"

Many musicians, such as Elvis Presley, Patsy Cline, Ray Charles, and Bob Dylan, have covered Nelson's tunes. In addition, a lot of movies and TV series have used his tunes.

Nelson draws inspiration for his songs from a multitude of sources, including his love of Texas, his own experiences as a songwriter, and great songwriters like Johnny Cash and Hank Williams. Nelson frequently writes songs on universal subjects like love, grief, and salvation.

Both fans and critics have applauded Nelson's songwriting. According to Rolling Stone, he is "one of the greatest songwriters of all time." Nelson, according to the New York Times, "is a master of the simple, catchy song."

His charitable work and activism

In addition, he has a strong philanthropic and activist side. Nelson has advocated for some causes, such as farm assistance, environmental preservation, and animal care, using his position to do so.

Agricultural Assistance
Nelson's involvement with Farm Aid, a nonprofit that raises funds and awareness to assist American family farmers, is arguably what has made him most well-known. In reaction to the farm crisis of the 1980s, which was brought on by some variables such as poor crop prices, high-interest rates, and a strong U.S. dollar, Nelson established Farm Aid in 1985. Millions of family farms were lost as a result of the crisis, and rural towns saw a downturn.

Nelson has supported Farm Aid nonstop from its inception. In addition to giving millions of dollars to Farm Aid, he has appeared in many of the organization's concerts. Nelson has also advocated for legislation that helps family farmers and rural communities by using his platform to speak out about the difficulties they face. Since 1985, Farm Aid has raised more than $60 million. In addition to helping farmers transition to sustainable farming practices, supporting farmers markets and other local food systems, and lobbying for policies that support family farmers and rural communities, the funds have been used to support family farmers in some ways. These ways include emergency relief for farmers affected by natural disasters or economic hardship.

Protection of the Environment
Nelson is a fervent supporter of environmental preservation as well. He has advocated against climate change and given financial assistance to numerous environmental groups. The Willie Nelson

and Friends Environmental Foundation was established by Nelson in 1990 to promote environmental advocacy and education. Nelson has also promoted environmental causes with his music. His 2008 CD American Classic included songs about environmental issues like water pollution and climate change. Along with working on environmental songs, Nelson has also collaborated with other musicians on tracks like "Rainbow Connection" with Jack Johnson and "Earth Mother Blues" with Bonnie Raitt.

Animal Concern
Nelson is a fervent supporter of animal welfare as well. He has denounced animal abuse and is a vegetarian. Nelson has additionally contributed to numerous animal welfare groups. He established the Willie Nelson and Friends Animal Rescue Foundation in 2007 intending to help neglected and abandoned animals by giving them food and shelter.

Nelson has also advocated for animal welfare causes through his music. His CD Heroes, which was released in 2012, included songs about animal welfare issues like animal abuse and the value of having compassion for animals. Along with contributing to songs on animal welfare, Nelson has also worked with other musicians on songs including "Pretty Paper" by Roy Orbison and "Cowboys Are Real" by Kacey Musgraves.

Other Reasons
Nelson has additionally backed some other causes, such as the legalization of drugs, and rights for Native Americans, and veterans. He has argued for social justice and peace while speaking out against violence and conflict. Nelson has also given millions of dollars to some foundations and charities.

Here are a few particular instances of Nelson's charitable giving and activism:

Nelson took part in a charity concert for American Indian activist Leonard Peltier, who was incarcerated, in 1987.

The Willie Nelson and Friends Environmental Foundation was established by Nelson in 1990 to promote environmental advocacy and education.

Nelson established the Willie Nelson and Friends Animal Rescue Foundation in 2007 intending to help injured and abandoned animals by giving them food and shelter.

Nelson's album Heroes, which was published in 2012, had songs regarding animal welfare issues such as animal abuse and the value of having compassion for animals.

Nelson established the Willie Nelson Alliance Against Homelessness in 2015, which offers assistance to veterans experiencing homelessness.

Nelson took part in a benefit event for Hurricane Harvey victims in 2017.
Nelson made a $1 million donation to the COVID-19 relief fund in 2020.
These are but a handful of Nelson's numerous charitable and activism pursuits. His work has truly changed the globe, and he is a true advocate of the people.

Chapter 6

Catalogs

A comprehensive rundown of all of Willie Nelson's studio, live, and compilation albums

Willie Nelson's Recorded Works

Over his career, Willie Nelson has put out over 70 studio albums. He has released CDs in many different genres, such as blues, jazz, folk, and country. Nelson is well-known for his unusual voice, easygoing demeanor, and knack for penning catchy yet thought-provoking songs.

Nelson's most well-known studio albums include a few of these:

Red Headed Stranger (1975): This record is regarded as one of the best-ever country records. Many of Nelson's beloved songs are featured on it, such as "Blue Eyes Crying in the Rain," "To All the Girls I've Loved Before," and "Sunday Morning Coming Down."

Nelson's 1978 CD Stardust includes his renditions of vintage pop tunes. It helped Nelson reach a wider audience and was a commercial and critical triumph.

Nelson and Waylon Jennings collaborated on the 1980 album Willie and the Wheel. It is regarded as one of the albums that most defined the outlaw country genre.

The album Always on My Mind (1982) marked Nelson's big break in the music industry. The album's lead single, which turned into one of Nelson's biggest hits, was included.

Nelson's 1993 CD Across the Borderline marked a return to his country music origins. Numerous duets with other country musicians, such as Emmylou Harris and Merle Haggard, were included.
Nelson has spent his entire career putting out new studio albums. In 2022, he published his most recent album, A Beautiful Time.

Live Records
Throughout his career, Nelson has also recorded more than a dozen live CDs. His live CDs are renowned for having a carefree and easygoing vibe. In between songs, Nelson frequently cracks jokes and stories that foster a sense of camaraderie among his followers.

Nelson's most well-known live CDs include a few of these:

Willie Nelson & Family Live (1971): Nelson performs with his family band on this record.

It's a wonderful illustration of Nelson's early live sound.

On the 1975 CD Willie Nelson and Pals Live & Kickin', Nelson performs alongside some of his pals, such as Waylon Jennings and Tom T. Hall. It embodies the sound of outlaw country music perfectly.

Across the Border: Live 1993 (1993): Nelson performs with several other country musicians on this CD, including Merle Haggard and Emmylou Harris. It is a superb illustration of Nelson's live sound from the nineties.

Live at Billy Bob's Texas (2005): This album showcases Nelson live in one of the biggest honky-tonks in the world, Billy Bob's Texas. It's a fantastic illustration of Nelson's live sound in the current day.

assemblages

Throughout his career, Nelson has also put out more than a dozen compilation CDs. A selection of Nelson's biggest successes and most well-known songs may be found on these albums.

Nelson's most well-known compilation albums include a few of these:

Greatest Hits (1973): Nelson's best-known songs from the 1960s and early 1970s are included on this CD.
A collection of Willie Nelson's biggest singles from the 1970s and early 1980s may be found on the album The Willie Nelson Collection (1984).
Willie Nelson's Greatest Hits (1989): Nelson's greatest hits from the 1960s to the late 1980s are included on this album.
The Crucial Willie Nelson (2003): This album includes some of Nelson's best-known songs from his entire discography.

Willie Nelson: American Outlaw (2014): This album offers a collection of Nelson's outlaw country songs.

Apart from his musical achievements, Nelson is an ardent activist who has utilized his position to garner support and awareness for an array of causes, such as animal welfare, environmental preservation, and farm assistance. Nelson is a genuine champion of the people, and the world has changed as a result of his actions.

Musical Heritage

Nelson has left a significant and enduring musical legacy. His songs have struck a chord with fans of all ages for many years, making him one of the most well-liked and respected characters in country music.

Hank Williams and Bob Wills, two traditional country and Western musicians, affected

Nelson's early music. Nelson did, however, also create his distinct sound, which was defined by his easygoing manner and unique voice.

Red Headed Stranger was Nelson's breakout album (1975). This record is regarded as one of the best country records ever released. Many of Nelson's beloved songs are featured on it, such as "Blue Eyes Crying in the Rain," "To All the Girls I've Loved Before," and "Sunday Morning Coming Down."

With albums like Stardust (1978), Willie and the Wheel (1980), and Always on My Mind (1982), Nelson's popularity persisted in the 1980s. These albums included Nelson's original songs, his collaborations with other country musicians, and his covers of beloved pop tunes.

Over his career, Nelson has persisted in putting out new music and going on frequent tours. In 2022, he published his most recent album, A Beautiful Time.

Many current country musicians, such as Miranda Lambert, Brad Paisley, and Garth Brooks, have drawn musical inspiration from Nelson. Many young musicians look up to Nelson because of his independent attitude and dedication to his work, making him a role model for them.

Legacy of Activism

In addition, Nelson is an ardent activist who has supported and promoted numerous causes using his platform.

Nelson established Farm Aid, a nonprofit that raises funds and public awareness to assist American family farmers, in 1985. Since Farm Aid's foundation, Nelson has been an unwavering supporter of the organization, helping to raise millions of dollars for it. Farm Aid concerts have also aided in advocating for policies that benefit family farmers and rural areas, as well as in bringing attention to the difficulties faced by these businesses.

Nelson is a fervent supporter of environmental preservation as well. He has advocated against climate change and given financial assistance to numerous environmental groups. Nelson has also promoted environmental causes with his music. For instance, his song "Rainbow Connection" was used in the 1992 animated picture FernGully: The Last Rainforest, which tells the story of a young fairy who goes to the rainforest to prevent it from being destroyed.

Nelson supports animal welfare as well. He has denounced animal abuse and is a vegetarian. Nelson has additionally contributed to numerous animal welfare groups. He has advocated for the advantages of medical marijuana, for instance, and serves as co-chair of the advisory board of the National Organization for the Reform of Marijuana Laws (NORML).

Nelson's world-changing advocacy has left a lasting impression. Millions of family farmers have been able to remain on the land because of Farm Aid. Nelson's support of environmental policy and environmental conservation has contributed to increasing public awareness of the issues affecting our world. Nelson's commitment to animal welfare has aided in the prevention of animal abuse as well as the advancement of more humane treatment of animals.

Appendix

Lyrics to some of Willie Nelson's most popular songs

Here are the lyrics to some of Willie
Nelson's most popular songs:

Always On My Mind

(Verse 1)
Maybe you'll think of me when you see the
The morning sunshine through the trees
And you'll know that I'm still in love with you
Maybe you'll think of me when you hear
A love song on the radio
And you'll know that I'll always be true

(Chorus)
Always on my mind
Always on my mind
You're always on my mind

And when I'm dreaming
You're always in my dreams
And when I'm waking
You're always on my mind

(Verse 2)
Maybe you'll think of me when you smell
The sweet perfume of a rose
And you'll know that I'm still in love with you
Maybe you'll think of me when you hear
The sound of children playing
And you'll know I'd love to have kids with you

(Chorus)
Always on my mind
Always on my mind
You're always on my mind
And when I'm dreaming
You're always in my dreams
And when I'm waking
You're always on my mind

(Bridge)

Always on my mind
Always on my mind
Always on my mind

On The Road Again

(Verse 1)
I'm on the road again
Just can't wait to get on the road again
The life I love is making music with my
friends
And I can't wait to get on the road again

(Chorus)
On the road again
Just can't wait to get on the road again
The life I love is making music with my
friends
And I can't wait to get on the road again

(Verse 2)
I see the world turning
As I'm on the road again
And I know where I belong

Willie Nelson

I'm on the road again

(Chorus)
On the road again
Just can't wait to get on the road again
The life I love is making music with my
friends
And I can't wait to get on the road again

Crazy

(Verse 1)
I'm crazy for loving you
I'm crazy for caring
I must be out of my mind
'Cause I'd do anything for you

(Chorus)
I'm crazy
I'm crazy
I'm crazy
I'm crazy for loving you

(Verse 2)

Willie Nelson

I'm crazy for thinking
That I could ever live without you
I'm crazy for needing
Everything you do

(Chorus)
I'm crazy
I'm crazy
I'm crazy
I'm crazy for loving you

(Bridge)
Oh, you make me crazy
For loving you
Crazy for loving you
Crazy for loving you

(Chorus)
I'm crazy
I'm crazy
I'm crazy
I'm crazy for loving you

Willie Nelson

I hope you enjoy the lyrics to these classic Willie Nelson songs!

Made in the USA
Columbia, SC
17 October 2024

44516117R00054